M000192181

The
PRAYER
of JABEZ

❧ LEADER'S GUIDE ❧

BRUCE
WILKINSON

Dear friend,

We've all been thrilled to experience a new movement sweep across our world—The Prayer of Jabez. The most amazing thing about this phenomenon is that it's based on a simple prayer that's been in our Bibles all along. All we needed to do was take a closer look at God's promises, and take Him at His word.

Now it's your turn to be a part of the miracle. As a Jabez group leader, you'll be the key to personal transformation in the lives of people close to you. It's one thing to watch the Jabez videos or read the book; it's another to take steps in faith to put truth into action—that's where you come in. You can encourage your people to claim God's blessings and expand their territory. You can coach and counsel them toward the fulfillment and ministry God wants them to have.

First and foremost, I hope you're already living the Jabez life. If you're praying the Jabez prayer every day, you already know the miracles that result—and you'll be that much more effective in leading your group toward lifechange.

Are you ready for a spiritual breakthrough in your group? Let's explore the prayer together!

Yours for blessing and service,

Bruce Wilkinson
President: Walk Thru the Bible International
Author: *The Prayer of Jabez*

Project Director: Dorit Radandt; Design: Randy Drake; Cover Design: Stephen Gardner; Curriculum Development David Wilkinson; Editor: Rob Suggs; Production: Lois Gable; Cover Photography: Photonica/Tatsuhiko Shimada

TABLE
of CONTENTS

LEADING THE PRAYER OF JABEZ VIDEO SERIES

Welcome to an adventure! Dr. Bruce Wilkinson's book The Prayer of Jabez has sparked a worldwide movement in which blessings and boundaries have grown. Now you have the opportunity to lead your group in a deeper encounter with the prayer. This Leader's Guide will walk you through all the steps to help make your experience unforgettable.

How Are The Sessions Designed?

The Prayer of Jabez has four sections: Bless me; Expand my territory; Put your hand on me; and Keep me from evil. The series includes two video sessions of approximately 30 minutes for each portion.

We've also included a third, non-video session for each section as an option to consider—a group discovery session to move your group deeper into the prayer. You might consider:

- **The Express Study:** 4 sessions—two video viewings in each meeting.
- **The Standard Study:** 8 sessions with video.
- **The Expanded Study:** 12 sessions including four group discovery sessions.

	Express (4 weeks)		Standard (8 weeks)		Expanded (12 weeks)
1	Bless Me Indeed!	1	Bless Me Indeed! (video)	1	Bless Me Indeed! A (video)
	A and B (video)	2	Bless Me Indeed! B (video)	2	Bless Me Indeed! B (video)
				3	Bless Me Indeed! (group)
2	Expand My Territory!	3	Expand My Territory! A (video)	4	Expand My Territory! A (video)
	A & B (video)	4	Expand My Territory! B (video)	5	Expand My Territory! B (video)
				6	Expand My Territory! (group)
3	Your Hand on Me!	5	Your Hand on Me! A (video)	7	Your Hand on Me! A (video)
	A & B (video)	6	Your Hand on Me! B (video)	8	Your Hand on Me! B (video)
				9	Your Hand on Me! (group)
4	Keep Me from Evil!	7	Keep Me from Evil! A (video)	10	Keep Me from Evil! A (video)
	A & B (video)	8	Keep Me from Evil! B (video)	11	Keep Me from Evil B (video)
				12	Keep Me from Evil! (group)

LEADING THE SESSIONS

As your group's leader, you have an exciting opportunity ahead. Many of your members will bring with them a great deal of familiarity and excitement about the prayer of Jabez. Some will already have experienced changed lives through the prayer. Take advantage of these factors and ask God to make your time together compelling and transforming. Use the prayer in your own daily devotions, asking God to change you and use you to change others.

You'll need to consider these major objectives as you prepare:

1. Choosing a time, place and format for holding the sessions.

2. Making arrangements for location and logistics.

3. Actively promoting and encouraging attendance.

4. Praying and preparing spiritually.

5. Leading successful sessions.

The following pages will offer some practical, helpful tips to make you an effective leader. But there's room for flexibility. Apply these guidelines to the specific situation of your group, whether in the classroom of a church, the home of a friend or the conference room of an office.

1

Choosing the Schedule and Format

- **Study the chart on the preceding page.** What kind of format will best meet your group's needs—the quick four-session "Express," the eight session "Standard" or the full, deluxe 12-session "Expanded" study? Decide which is best for your group and situation.

- **Plan the wisest use of time.** Video sessions last approximately 30 minutes, but your group time is a variable. Adapt our activity suggestions to fit your balance of time. Advance preparation on your part is essential.

  You need to decide exactly how much time you want to give to each question and each activity.

LEADING
THE SESSIONS

2

For the Sunday School Class

☐ **2 months before the sessions.** Call and write class members. Carefully explain the series and its purpose. Begin building excitement by spreading the word through the church.

☐ **1 month before the sessions.** Meet with your team to pray and plan. Use posters, flyers, and bulletin inserts to spread the word.

☐ **2 weeks before the sessions.** Contact members again. Make a list of details to check, including room availability, a good VCR and monitor, workbooks, etc. Spend extra time in daily prayer.

For the Home Group

☐ **1 month before the sessions.** Call and write group members. Ask them to consider bringing a friend. Begin talking consistently and excitedly about the series.

☐ **2 weeks before the sessions.** Discuss the importance of the series with your members. Check VCR, materials, etc. Send out cards inviting friends to your Jabez group. Pray daily.

For the Church or Large Group Format

☐ **3 months before the sessions.** Write key church or organizational leaders. Provide information to them. Use posters, flyers, and local advertising to promote your seminar.

☐ **2 months before the sessions.** At church, begin promoting the seminars from the pulpit during worship. Check course materials, room availability, refreshment plans, and other logistics. Delegate jobs to workers—greeting, refreshments, follow-up, etc.

☐ **1 week before the sessions.** Plan a final phone blitz. Make final checks on logistics. Use signs and be sure visitors can find the room. Schedule a special prayer meeting.

Maximize Session Time

Create an effective learning environment

- **Arrange the room.** Are the chairs in the best place for viewing the video? Is the monitor set up to avoid window glare? For large groups, procure a video projector or large-screen television.

- **Name tags** are always a good idea. Provide tags and bold pens. Arrange for a friendly host or hostess to greet people as they arrive. Also, have extra pencils for note-taking.

- **Refreshments** help the fellowship factor and build a comfortable and responsive group. Have light refreshments before or after your meeting, as it suits your particular arrangement.

Prepare for the Session.

- **Pray hard—before, during and after the seminars.** Pray for individuals. This is your most important preparation.

- **Know the content.** Go over the video and notebook material. Prepare for likely questions.

- **Be transformed by the material,** and be prepared to share how the Jabez prayer has impacted your life.

Keep it moving without rushing.

- **Balance time management with sensitive group dynamics.** Cover the material, but be flexible enough to deal with your group's needs as the Spirit leads you.

- **Don't be sidetracked.** If it a member's question is complex, handle it after the session or privately during the week. Keep the whole group in mind.

Be personable and responsive.

- **Know names!** Keep a list of participants, make notes and review during the week. Greet people by name; it makes a difference!

- **Build group chemistry.** Help people interact and get to know each other.

PERSONALIZE YOUR SESSION

- **One-Hour Sessions.** If you use a 60-minute format, you'll have slightly less than 30 minutes for the balance of activities after the video. Carefully guide the interaction. Encourage people to arrive early. Delay prayer requests, and announcements for the final moments. Use questions that encourage short answers. Use small group time, dividing quickly and providing one key question for discussion. See the chart below.

- **Ninety minutes or longer.** Lengthier sessions provide greater flexibility. You'll be able to build more quality and depth into small group times. You'll also have more time available for questions, deeper topic exploration, and prayer. See the chart below.

- **Optional Workshop Weeks.** This book includes material for extra sessions for each of the four parts of the Jabez prayer. This session would use no video, but devote the time to group interaction in "workshop" style. This is strongly recommended if time permits.

Video lengths vary from 30 to 35 minutes.
Time Allotments for 60- and 90-Minute Sessions

	For One-Hour Session...	For a 90-Minute Session...
Introduce the session.	5 minutes total	15 minutes total
• Greet the group.	2 minutes	5 minutes
• Introduce the video.	3 minutes	5 minutes
• Build the need.	------------	5 minutes
Play the Video.	Allow 35 minutes.	Allow 35 minutes.
Interact with the group.	20 minutes total	40 minutes total
• Summarize the "Big Idea."	2 minutes	3 minutes
• Question and answer.	6 minutes	8 minutes
• Interaction in smaller groups.	6 minutes	20 minutes
• Give a homework assignment.	1 minutes	1 minutes
• Prayer time.	5 minutes	8 minutes

BLESS ME INDEED!

Leader's Checklist

☐ I've prayed for the session intensely.

☐ I've planned for the session thoroughly.

☐ I've studied the material carefully.

☐ I've been changed by the material personally.

1. Introduce the session

• **Greet the group.** Let your eagerness show. Members can introduce themselves or share one goal they have for their study of the Prayer.

• **Introduce the concept.** Ask: "What's the first word that comes to mind when you hear the word 'blessing'? Why?" Give members a moment to process this question.

• **Build the need.** Ask: "Have you ever considered the goodness of God? Considering that, have you wondered if He might have something really wonderful in store for you, and it's just a matter of asking Him for it? Today could open the door toward God's blessings for your life in a new and exciting way."

2. Play the Video (Course Workbook pages 9-11)

Allow 35 minutes for Dr. Wilkinson's video presentation. Make the sure the volume is sufficient, and that everyone has a good view.

Watch for the Big Idea: God is more loving than we can imagine, and He loves nothing better than to bless His children. He has blessings for each member of your group. When we call for them intensely, He blesses us generously.

When the video has concluded, ask for questions and comments. Some will want to know the words that fill in certain blanks in their workbooks. Take care of this so it won't divert attention.

3. Guide the Discussion

Note: Leaders should adapt this material to fit the time available.
Consult the first section of this book for time allotments.

1. What was the greatest "aha!" idea you received from Dr. Wilkinson's presentation?

2. What questions did the presentation raise in your mind?

Divide the group into units of two or three. Direct them to the discussion questions on page 12 of the video workbook. Please use these comments on the questions from the workbook to help guide the discussion.

Question 1 directs your members to consider the blessings of their past. They'll discover that some blessings were "earned," while others were gifts of love. God's blessings parallel this principle.

Question 2. Most members will be willing to admit, having considered the video material, that they haven't taken advantage of the love God wants to offer. They are then given the opportunity to consider how to begin doing that.

Question 3 None of us can fully comprehend the extent of God's goodness. Most of us have sadly inadequate views of Him. Give your group members time to confront this crucial question of the nature and character of God.

Question 4 also provides an effective vehicle for considering the overwhelming love of God. This powerful passage, Matthew 7:7–11, shows Him as the loving parent. If there are parents in your group, ask them to reflect upon their own delight in blessing their children.

Bring your full group back together for the final question.

Question 5 This question places us in the presence of the Father Himself and dares us to imagine the blessings He might have in store for our lives. This concludes your session with the compelling directive to go after God's blessings. Build the scene. Have your group members close their eyes and imagine themselves in God's presence. Direct them in prayer.

Homework Group members should spend time with God during the week, praising Him for His goodness and asking for blessings. Next week they'll be asked to report what happened.

BLESS ME INDEED!

1. Introduce the session

• **Greet the group.** Welcome everyone back. Ask a member to share his or her greatest insight from last week. Ask members to report on their homework assignment.

• **Introduce the concept.** Ask: "What would life look like for any of us, if we lived the blessed life every day? What if our whole group lived that life?" Give members a moment to process this question.

• **Build the need.** Ask: "Have you ever considered the possibility that there are different varieties of blessings, rather than merely one kind? If you knew what they were, couldn't you seek them better? Today we'll unlock God's storehouse and find what treasures await there!"

2. Play the Video (Course Workbook pages 15-17)

Allow 35 minutes for the video presentation. Make sure the volume is sufficient, and that everyone has a good view.

Watch for the Big Idea: The blessed life is an adventure. It's available to every single one of us, because God loves each of us infinitely. Deeper joy and deeper fulfillment are just within reach.

When the video has concluded, ask for questions and comments. Help them fill in blanks in their workbooks.

3. Guide the Discussion

Before this week's session, evaluate the flow and effectiveness of your first one. Did you have enough time? Did you spend too much time in any segment? Reflect and adjust

1. Last week we learned exciting things about the character of God. How does that lead us into the central point of today's presentation?

2. Which type of blessing from God means the most to you? Why?

Divide the group into units of two or three. Direct them to the discussion questions on page 18 of the video workbook. These comments on the questions from the workbook should help you guide the discussion.

Question 1 Quickly summarize last week's insight into God's character. The first question looks back to that session and also calls on your members to think about creation as a blessing from God. Everyone will enjoy naming their favorite blessing from creation.

Question 2 Many people equate "blessing" with "gift"—for example birthday gifts. Remind your group that a blessing can be a word of encouragement, an opportunity, and an honor. Review the definition of the word at the beginning of the first session.

Question 3 turns the tables. Have we blessed others? Part of the blessed life is being a blessing-giver. This may provide a flash of insight for many of your members. Challenge them to bless someone each day in the coming week.

Question 4 Think about the difference between "striving for" blessings and "enjoying" them. This is a compelling point. Do you know how to simply enjoy God and delight in Him? How might that affect the way God blesses you? How does a child's obvious enjoyment affect the parent's willingness to bless them?

Bring your full group back together for the final question

Question 5 again provides us with a scenario to visualize. Help your group members create this mental picture. What kinds of blessings would be there? How would they respond emotionally? What would they be likely to say? As leader, be sure you personally reflect on this idea.

Homework This week your group members should make a written "blessing inventory" and update it daily. Encourage them to identify every blessing they receive—and also those they give.

BLESS ME INDEED!

Optional Group Discovery Session

Group Discovery sessions may be the most life-changing of all. Be sure to select dependable group leaders. Keep all groups on schedule to complete the tasks.

Leader's Checklist
☐ I've prayed for the session intensely.
☐ I've planned for the session thoroughly.
☐ I've studied the material carefully.
☐ I've been changed by the material personally.

1. Introduce the session

• **Greet the group.** Tell them something special is planned for this session—an opportunity to dig deeper in Jabez blessings and apply them to their lives.

• **Build the need.** Ask: "What if you could draft a blueprint for a new kind of life—a life of daily blessings and godly abundance? Would you like to try doing so today?"

2. Divide into small groups

• Place your members in units of three or four members each. These groups will be retained for all four Group Discovery sessions.

• Pray for everyone. Ask God's Spirit to guide each group into exciting discoveries.

3. Reviewing the Jabez Blessing

• Move quickly through the main points of the first two sessions. Some may have missed one or even both sessions. Review both sessions over a few minutes.

4. What's your BQ (Blessing Quotient)?

Group members should be given this scale for discussion, and to determine their location:

1—I receive no blessings in life, and I offer none.

2—I'm aware of the basic blessings of creation, but few personally.

3—God has blessed me, but I know there could be so much more.

4—I tend to be aware of daily blessings; I seek them; I bless others.

5—My life is based on God's plentiful blessings—and I'm committed to being a blessing.

Optional Group Discovery Session

- **Everyone should discuss:**

a) What factors helped them reach their "BQ"?

b) What factors have been obstacles to moving forward?

c) What steps would help them break through to the next level?
   Answers should be written on paper as well as shared aloud.

5. Discovering the Word: Jabez Blessings
Turn to page 34 in your Prayer of Jabez Workbook.

- **Ephesians 1:3 – 14.** Read this passage together, also using the workbook's summary. Discuss the rich and varied blessings of the Jabez life. This is a study of the depth and power of the blessings God has already made available to us.

- **Questions 2 and 3.** Be certain you explore each of this passage's blessings. Your group members need to understand how each of them apply to their lives. These questions will help you accomplish that goal; they're the heart of this study.

- **Questions 4.** Take note of the phrase, "to the praise of His glory," which occurs twice in the passage. The meaning is that we live completely for the glory of God; his blessings show the world His goodness and glory. Try to use personal illustrations.

- **Questions 5.** Apply the deep spiritual truth in this passage to the everyday issues your people face. Lead them to discuss how to live the blessed life. By the time you finish, your group members should have a rich understanding of God's blessings "in the heavenly places"—and they can reach for more blessings to the glory of the Father.

6. Praying Together
Leave sufficient time for group prayer at the end of your session. Point out that that the purpose of blessings is to know, enjoy and serve God better.

Homework This week your group members should make a written "blessing inventory" and update it daily. Encourage them to identify every blessing they receive—and also those they give. Encourage each member to do something that blesses someone else each day.

ENLARGE MY TERRITORY!

1. Introduce the session

• **Greet the group with excitement.** Refer to the impact of the previous sessions.

• **Introduce the concept.** Say: "Last week you were asked why blessings would lead to this second part of the Prayer: 'Enlarge my territory.' What have you decided?"

• **Build the need.** Ask: "Have you ever wished you could be a person of greater influence? How would you like to double your impact? Triple it? Today we'll discover how people all over the world are doing that through the Prayer of Jabez."

2. Play the Video (Course Workbook pages 21-23)

Allow 35 minutes for the video presentation. As always, check that everyone is happy with the volume and their view.

Watch for the Big Idea: God never desires that we stand still. He wants us always moving forward and outward in ministry—and that applies to every single one of us. We need only ask Him to expand our territory, then be open to the places and directions where He expands it.

When the video has concluded, ask for questions and comments. Offer the answers to blanks they missed. Help everyone make the transition to the next activity.

3. Guide the Discussion

Always watch to be certain you're staying close to your allotted time

1. In your opinion, what is the greatest misconception people have about this portion of the Jabez prayer? Why do they have that misunderstanding?

2. How many of you feel that God is already enlarging your territory—and know where He is enlarging it? (*Simply ask for a show of hands; people can discuss the specifics later.*)

Divide the group into units of two or three. Direct them to the discussion questions on page 24 of the video workbook. Let these comments on the questions from the workbook help guide your discussion.

Question 1 Before the meeting, be certain paper and pencils are available for this exercise. Help your group members think of the various kinds of "territory" in each of our lives. Encourage them to discuss their circles with the rest of the group.

Question 2 The essence of this question is this: we need never fear God's work in our lives. He prepares and equips us for the tasks He gives us. Serving Him is joyful and fulfilling. Just the same, people assume God will send them somewhere they don't want to go.

Question 3 Though it's exciting and rewarding to move to higher levels in life, it's frightening and challenging, too—at least at first. It helps to realize we've already risen to a few challenges previously, and it felt good to do so.

Question 4 This question moves us toward the specific issue of the key area in which God wants to enlarge our work. Many of your group members will have already given this question a great deal of thought. Allow plenty of time for discussion here.

Bring your full group back together for the final question

Question 5 Your group members will quickly identify with the idea of "border bullies". It's very important to take time to "see" these enemies and especially put names to them, calling them for what they are. This should be a moment of clarification and commitment.

Homework Be certain your members have written down the names of the "border bullies" who would prevent them from going where God wants them to go. Ask them to spend the week reflecting and praying about God's power which can overcome anything. Challenge them to make a clear breakthrough this week in that area.

ENLARGE MY TERRITORY!

1. Introduce the session

• **Greet the group.** Welcome everyone back. We're in the second half of "Enlarge My Territory"—the heart of the Jabez prayer. Say a word about the great things God is doing through our study.

• **Introduce the concept.** Say: "Life can be seen as a series of struggles to break through to higher levels— through childhood, into adolescence, into adulthood, marriage, parenting, careers. Our "territories" are always changing—and God wants us to be victorious."

• **Build the need.** Ask: "Can you feel God calling you onward today? He certainly is doing so. What would it feel like to step through the door today, and move into the new kind of life He wants for you—a life of impact and daily victory? Let's find out about that kind of life."

2. Play the Video (Course Workbook pages 27-29)

Allow 35 minutes for the video presentation.

Watch for the Big Idea: There are specific and identifiable ways that God enlarges our territory. When we see what is involved, how it feels, and what the results will be, we can't say no! This is life's greatest adventure.

When the video has concluded, ask for questions and comments. Help them fill in blanks in their workbooks.

3. Guide the Discussion

Make the transition from passive viewing to active discussion. Use these questions to get people talking.

1. Last week we discussed "border bullies". Did you experience a breakthrough during the week? (*Select one person to share their experience.*)

2. As you think about the territory God has for every one of us, what one word comes to your mind? Why?

Divide the group into units of two or three. Direct them to the discussion questions on page 30 of the video workbook. Let these comments help guide your discussion.

Question 1 To reply to this question, people will need to identify the area in which God wants to enlarge their territory. Ask people to state the "where" before they consider the "how." You might allow each group member to reply.

Question 2. This question will require much thought for most people. Give them a moment to consider. Not everyone will have a reply, but it's important that everyone reflects on the issue of neglected gifts; God loves using them in surprising ways.

Question 3 This question inspires deep emotion in many of us. We all struggle for breakthrough at times. Members should use this time to encourage each other to move forward where they feel God calling them. Let them exchange advice and pray for one another.

Question 4 Give your members a moment to list these areas, then determine which ones would best serve God's kingdom purposes. The latter portion of the question sets up our final reflection and homework assignment.

Bring your full group back together for the final question

Question 5 Group members should be asked to pull together all their insights from the preceding four questions, as well as the video presentation, then determine what God wants the next step to be. Their replies shouldn't be general, but one specific action that can be taken.

Homework With respect to Question 5, take one giant step this week. Focus on the area in which you can best push out your borders for God, then make your move this week. This week could bring the turning point of your life!

Extra Session
Non-Video
Course Workbook page 35

ENLARGE MY TERRITORY!

Optional Group Discovery Session

If you're using these Group Discovery sessions, you know how powerful they can be. Keep the tasks on schedule, but be flexible to what God is doing in the hearts of your people.

Leader's Checklist

☐ I've prayed for the session intensely.

☐ I've planned for the session thoroughly.

☐ I've studied the material carefully.

☐ I've been changed by the material personally.

1. Introduce the session

• **Greet the group.** We're at the mid-point of the Jabez Adventure! God is doing great things. Be sure you communicate all the joy and excitement with which you began.

• **Build the need.** Ask: "What if you held in your hands the action plan for your life—and it showed how to experience joy and victory you never imagined? Be ready to work, because we're going to try to draw up that plan for enlarging our territory."

2. Divide into small groups

• Place your members in units of three or four members each. If possible, use the same groups as Session One / group interaction. Help newcomers find and adjust to groups.

• Pray for everyone. Ask God's Spirit to guide each group into life-change.

3. Reviewing the Jabez Territory

• Move quickly through the main points of the first two sessions. Some may have missed one or both sessions. Review the "Big Ideas" briefly.

4. What's your TQ (Territory Quotient)?

Group members should be given this scale to discuss and identify their status:

1—I have no idea what God wants me to do in life.

2—I agree God wants more for me, but I understand only the general ideas of where.

3—God is giving me new horizons all the time, but I need a big breakthrough.

4—I'm right at the border of a huge breakthrough to a life of godly impact.

5—I'm even now breaking through to the greatest, most thrilling challenge I've ever had.

Optional Group Discovery Session

- **Everyone should discuss:**
  a) What factors helped them reach their "BQ"?
  b) What factors have been obstacles to moving forward?
  c) What steps would help them break through to the next level?
     Answers should be written on paper as well as shared aloud.

5. Discovering the Word: Jabez Borders

Turn to page 35 in your Prayer of Jabez Workbook.

- **Deuteronomy 1:6 – 8.** Read this passage together; refer to the workbook's summary. You might want to review with your group why the Israelites wandered for nearly 40 years. The Israelites' "Border Bullies" were referred to as "giants in the land" (see the first question). Explain this point. Ask your group member to identify their personal "giants."

- **Question 2.** There are many factors. Help your members think of their own situations.

- **Questions 3.** Group members need to see that God sets goals in our sight. We can always see (if we're willing) where He wants us to go. This should motivate us into action.

- **Questions 4.** "You have dwelt long enough at this mountain," God told His people. The point here is for your people to understand what their comfort zone is, so they can move out of it. Encourage your group members to share honestly, so others can encourage them.

- **Questions 5.** Now we've "talked the talk." This question directs us to "walk the walk." Ask your group members to make a personal commitment, and hold each other accountable to carrying it out—even if only in a small way—in the coming week.

6. Praying Together

Leave time for prayer. Focus on the fact that God is performing miracles in the lives of many in this room. As the leader, you should close the prayer. Call on God to perform miracles in the coming week.

Homework Affirm that we're all going to be overwhelmed with the challenges God gives us. That's what the next part of the prayer is about. Everyone should ask God to empower them in the coming week so they can report about it in the next session.

PUT YOUR HAND ON ME!

1. Introduce the session

• **Greet the group.** If possible, begin with a quick word about the personal impact this course has had on your life. Express your anticipation of the miracles still to come.

• **Introduce the concept.** Ask: "Have you ever had that moment of moving on to something new and exciting—then realizing you're in over your head? It happens when we serve God, too—that's why we rely on His power."

• **Build the need.** Ask: "Are you struggling with various limits and barriers right now? What if you found the key to rising above the things that keep you from reaching your goals? God makes it very clear that we can find that key. Listen closely to discover what it is."

2. Play the Video (Course Workbook pages 41-43)

Allow 35 minutes for the video presentation.

Watch for the Big Idea: Without God's empowerment, we'll never accomplish the greatest goals of life. We feel His hand when we have the willingness to do His work. He yearns to pour out His power upon every one of us.

When the video has concluded, ask for questions and comments. Don't forget to help your group members fill in the blanks they missed.

3. Guide the Discussion

Note: This session in particular provokes vivid discussion and questions. Most people are fascinated with the power of God. Allow free discussion, but stay on task and keep things moving. Monitor your time.

1. For you, what was the most surprising statement Dr. Wilkinson made about God's hand?

2. Why do you think so few people ever really feel the hand of God on their life?

Divide the group into units of two or three. Direct them to the discussion questions on page 44 of the video workbook. Please use these comments to guide the discussion.

Question 1 This serves as a good "ice-breaker" question, because it allows people to reflect on the central question without having to share personal information. As leader be prepared to give an example of a godly person you know.

Question 2 Some may not know many biblical illustrations, but the point is clear—the Spirit of God always brings self-control. There are various reasons people ascribe a loss of control to God's power: New Age and other beliefs, fear, ignorance, and unbiblical models.

Question 3 This question requires study of the Scriptures. Be certain Bibles are available. The point here is that God judges unbelief. If we don't take the power of God seriously, we'll never be capable of serving Him to the fullest. And it is a deep problem in our modern age.

Question 4 This question will be discussed in terms (what God seeks in people) but your group members will be measuring themselves against God's standards. This is a very important moment of self-evaluation. God doesn't seek perfection, but commitment and availability.

Bring your full group back together for the final question.

Question 5 Be sensitive to the fact that some have never felt God's hand in their lives. Still, this is a challenge. You may want to bring this session to a close with a brief testimony about your own life and how it felt when "God showed up." Group members should leave with a powerful yearning to move forward in the power of God.

Homework Challenge your group members to seek God's power this week as never before. Remind them that it doesn't come in a vacuum, but when we're actually serving Him. They should pray each day for an opportunity to use God's power in God's service.

PUT YOUR HAND ON ME!

1. Introduce the session

• **Greet the group.** Welcome everyone back. Ask if anyone felt the hand of God as they served Him this week. Allow them to share for a moment.

• **Introduce the concept.** Ask: "What does it look like when God's hand rests upon you or me? (You might refer here to the testimony just given.) There are certain signs that God is present and moving."

• **Build the need.** Say: "If you're like me, you've read about 'great Christians' for many years. You've longed for that kind of life. You've yearned for the hand of God upon you. Would you like to discover how it can happen? Dr. Wilkinson will tell us in this video."

2. Play the Video (Course Workbook pages 47-49)

Allow 35 minutes for the video presentation.

Watch for the Big Idea: God may move in mysterious ways, but there's a lot we can know for certain about His hand. It always moves in certain ways, and it rests upon us when we do certain things. They're enumerated in this presentation.

When the video has concluded, ask for questions and comments.

3. Guide the Discussion

As always, keep control of the proceedings. Let people share, but don't let particular individuals monopolize the discussion.

1. We've seen that God's hand intervenes in certain situations. When have you an example of one of the situations Dr. Wilkinson described?

2. Which is the hardest of the four practical steps to experiencing God's power?

Divide the group into units of two or three. Direct them to the discussion questions on page 50 of the video workbook. Use these comments to guide the discussion.

Question 1 Being totally dependent upon God's hand can be frightening! But the results make it all worthwhile. Many people will think of a time when God came through for them, perhaps during a crisis. Try to emphasize situations of moving out aggressively in ministry.

Question 2. This is a crucial point about the fine line between faith and impulsiveness. All through the Jabez experience is the issue of asking, but waiting. God blesses us, enlarges us, and empowers us in His way, not ours. Be certain your people are clear on this point.

Question 3 In the case of questions alluding to biblical stories, be certain you review the stories before the session. This particular question offers several encouraging examples of the fact that God never sends us out alone to do His work. This alone is enough to dispel our fear.

Question 4 Many people are "stretching the muscle" of faith more than ever before in their Jabez journeys. Expect them to relate what God is doing in their lives right now. Encourage them that, it's always demanding and tiring to build up muscles, it's the same way with faith. But it's great to be strong!

Bring your full group back together for the final question.

Question 5 This is a difficult question. Let people from the assembled group offer pointers in how we can know we're truly walking in faith. Suggestions: biblical precedent, prayerful confirmation, the approval of our authorities, support of Christian friends, and common sense.

Homework By this stage in the Jabez adventure, we're all very different people from the ones we were at the beginning. This week, take time to reflect on how far God has brought you, and where you think He's leading you. Write down your observations. Spend time praising Him, and write out your goals for the months ahead.

Extra Session
Non-Video
Course Workbook page 36

PUT YOUR HAND ON ME!

Optional Group Discovery Session

As always, be aware that God's Spirit is present and working deeply in the lives of your people. Pray deeply and individually for your group members as you prepare for this session.

Leader's Checklist

- ☐ I've prayed for the session intensely.
- ☐ I've planned for the session thoroughly.
- ☐ I've studied the material carefully.
- ☐ I've been changed by the material personally.

1. Introduce the session

- **Greet the group.** Thank everyone for returning for another opportunity to dig deeper into the Jabez life and become more committed to what God is doing.

- **Build the need.** Ask: "Are you ready to discover the power of God in your life? We've learned a great deal about it, but wouldn't your really like to experience it? During this time of group discovery, you have an opportunity of discussing the hand of God on you."

2. Divide into small groups

- Place your members in their usual groups, or in appropriate groupings.
- Pray for everyone. Ask God's Spirit to guide each group into exciting discoveries.

3. Reviewing the Jabez "Hand of God"

- Move quickly through the main points of the first two sessions, remembering that some may have missed a session. Today's effectiveness is dependent upon our past studies.

4. What's your PQ (Power Quotient)?

Group members should be given this scale for discussion, and to determine where they stand:

1—The power of God isn't moving through me at all.

2—I know God's Spirit lives in my heart, but I rarely experience His hand on me.

3—I've had moments when God used me, but only occasionally.

4—God's hand is on me quite often; the purpose of my life is to live in His power.

5—I feel that God's hand is upon me regularly, and I'm ministering for Him.

Optional Group Discovery Session

- **Everyone should discuss:**

a) What factors helped them reach their "PQ"?

b) What factors have been obstacles to moving forward?

c) What steps would help them break through to the next level?
Answers should be written on paper as well as shared aloud.

5. Discovering the Word: Jabez Power

Turn to page 36 in your Prayer of Jabez Workbook.

- **John 14:12 – 18.** Discuss how amazing it is that Jesus would promise that we might outdo His miracles! Discuss the outline offered in the third paragraph on the workbook page (1. Believe. 2. Ask. 3. Obey.) Faith is the first essential, then we must ask God to move in power; and we must be willing to be obedient to His direction.

- **Question 2.** The key, according to Jesus, is asking in the name of Jesus, which demonstrates we're acting on His behalf, to glorify God.

- **Questions 3.** There is no way we can serve God without following His commandments. Obedience proves we are truly serving Him. Faith and obedience activate His mighty power.

- **Questions 4.** It's encouraging to know that the Spirit, who empowers us, also helps us and comforts us. He gives us practical support (power) and emotional support (love).

- **Questions 5.** Again, we're left with the motivation that comes in knowing God never sends us out alone. Throughout Scripture we're told He will go with us. Tell your members that as they do God's work, it's as if He is standing beside them. This is a positive and powerful note on which to conclude your discussion.

6. Praying Together

As you've sensed what God is doing through the small groups in this session, have a time of expressing back to Him the praise and excitement you feel.

Homework Challenge group members to take their "action steps" and trust God for the victory. In the next session they'll have the opportunity to tell the group what happened.

KEEP ME FROM EVIL!

Leader's Checklist

- ☐ I've prayed for the session intensely.
- ☐ I've planned for the session thoroughly.
- ☐ I've studied the material carefully.
- ☐ I've been changed by the material personally.

1. Introduce the session

- **Greet the group.** We approach the culmination of our Jabez adventure. Great things have occurred, and greater ones are within reach! Encourage and energize your group.

- **Introduce the concept.** Say: "With great power comes great responsibility. The greater our service, the greater our temptations. That's why Jabez asked God to keep him from evil."

- **Build the need.** Say: "If you are a member of the human race, you are struggling with temptation right now. You know you could serve God—but what if you stumble? How would you like to have protection from evil? Let's find out how to do that."

2. Play the Video (Course Workbook pages 53-55)

Allow 35 minutes for the video presentation.

Watch for the Big Idea: God can and will protect us from various types of evil, but as we've discovered throughout the Jabez experience—we have to ask!

When the video has concluded, ask for questions and comments. Don't forget to help your group members fill in the blanks they missed.

3. Guide the Discussion

As we study the prayer, "Bless Me" gives us joy; "Enlarge My Territory" gives us vision; "Put Your Hand On Me" gives us excitement; and "Keep Me From Evil" gives us protection. Many of your group members will be confronted by conviction in this session. Be sensitive to the inner struggles that may not be verbalized.

1. The final portion of Jabez's prayer concerns evil. Why didn't he put this at the beginning?

2. If God's hand is upon you, why would you need to be more aware of evil? Explain.

Divide the group into units of two or three. Direct them to the discussion questions on page 56 of the video workbook. Use these comments to guide the group discussion.

Question 1 There may be an infinite number of possible answers to this question. The purpose is to get your group thinking about the variety of temptations and sins we may face. We can't know, of course, which ones Jabez encountered—but we know he had to face sin just as we do.

Question 2. Jesus and Jabez both asked God to keep them from evil, but most of us are not so wise. One possible answer is arrogance; we think we don't need to ask. Praying the Jabez prayer each day sharpens our awareness of temptation and insures that we'll follow God's guidance to avoid evil.

Question 3 The most basic sins, of course, never change—pride, greed, lust, and so on. Our sin creates a barrier that keeps us from breaking through to the larger territory He wants to give us, or from feeling the power of His hand. There are many biblical examples.

Question 4 This question could draw hours of responses! Take care that it doesn't turn into a "venting" session. The important point is to observe the extensive damage done by any form of sin, and to see the "domino effect" that begins when sin enters our lives.

Bring your full group back together for the final question.

Question 5 Underline this point as powerfully as you can. As in our previous sessions, give your group members a mental image—one of God encircling them, limiting the scope and power of the sin that would entangle us. If we know this, we feel stronger. Through God's power we can stand up to any temptation that stands in our way.

Homework As you close, ask your group members to close their eyes and call to mind the one greatest temptation they continue to face. Ask them to hand it over to God in their minds and hearts. Challenge them to expect God to give them a victory over it for this week.

KEEP ME FROM EVIL!

1. Introduce the session

• **Greet the group.** This is our final video session. Challenge the group to let God make it the best of all in the transformation of their lives.

• **Introduce the concept.** Say: "The world may change, but evil never does. The devil's strategies are the same now as they ever were—and that means we can study his battle plan."

• **Build the need.** Ask: "If you could see yourself through the devil's eyes, and know how he was going to try tripping you up, how would it affect your day? Today you'll have the opportunity to catch a glimpse of his strategy for your life—and the result will change the way you live your life!"

2. Play the Video (Course Workbook pages 59-61)

Allow 35 minutes for the video presentation.

Watch for the Big Idea: Evil and temptation are so very deadly, yet God's love is so overpowering. We must know how the enemy works, but we must also know how the Father overcomes.

When the video has concluded, ask for questions and comments.

3. Guide the Discussion

Ask the Spirit to move within the room as your group confronts the dangers of temptation and the deliverance of God.

1. Do you think there are countless varieties of sin, or only a few that never change? Why?

2. What do you believe is the single most hopeful truth for us to remember as we face evil?

You might want to stay together for the first question, then divide the group into units of two or three for the following ones. Use the discussion questions on page 62 of the video workbook. Use these comments to guide your discussion.

Question 1 This first exercise will require paper, and you may want to do it as a larger group, since some will not wish to discuss their answers. Give them a minute to reflectively prioritize their lists, then dismiss everyone to the smaller groups.

Question 2. The second question can more comfortably be discussed by groups. We can't know the correct answers, of course. The point is that the devil uses all of these constantly, and we need to be alert.

Question 3 Temptations change as we change. For example, if we attain more influence over others, pride may become a greater danger. Other temptations remain basic in relation to our weak spots.

Question 4 God speaks to us and strengthens us spiritually through His Word. Avoiding the Bible affects the spirit as starving affects the body. We can't afford to lower our defenses when contemplating the power of temptation—so we must be disciplined in prayer and God's Word.

Bring your full group back together for the final question.

Question 5 The entire group should be given a few moments to begin reviewing their notes to see the points they found most compelling and life-changing. They might want to list ten of those—or more. Encourage them not to finish this task at home, in the assignment below.

Homework All group members should complete the lists of important points from the Jabez course. On one side of the page, they should write out the point. On the other side, they should name the specific life-change this point is bringing about in their lives. They should keep these lists, check them frequently, and ask God to keep transforming them more to the image of Christ with every new day.

KEEP ME FROM EVIL!

Optional Group Discovery Session

This is the final Jabez session of all. Make it the most challenging and motivating. Try to save some time to allow people to share how the Prayer of Jabez has changed their lives.

Leader's Checklist

- ☐ I've prayed for the session intensely.
- ☐ I've planned for the session thoroughly.
- ☐ I've studied the material carefully.
- ☐ I've been changed by the material personally.

1. Introduce the session

- **Greet the group.** Welcome them to final Jabez group discovery meeting. But remind them that this is really only the beginning of many miracles God will bring to their lives.

- **Build the need.** Ask: "How would you like to pull it all together—God's blessings, His enlargement of our territory, His hand upon us, and His protection from evil? What would it mean to live out the prayer every day? Let's explore it deeper in our final session."

2. Divide into small groups

- Place your members in their usual groups, or in appropriate groupings.

- Pray for everyone. Ask God's Spirit to guide each group into exciting discoveries.

3. Reviewing the Jabez "Keep Me from Evil"

- Review the main points of the first two sessions on temptation. Also give a broad review of the four major points of the prayer, showing how each one leads to the next.

4. What's your RQ (Resistance Quotient)?

Group members should be given this scale for discussion, and to determine where they stand:

1—I feel totally incapable of overcoming my struggles with temptation.

2—I've overcome temptation in the past, but lack a sense of God's power.

3—I struggle daily and often fail, I'm learning to trust God in temptation.

4—I've begun to see victory my struggles, and trust God more each day.

5—I ask God to keep me from evil each day, and I feel my spiritual strength increasing.

Optional Group Discovery Session

- **Everyone should discuss:**

a) What factors helped them reach their "RQ"?

b) What factors have been obstacles to moving forward?

c) What steps would help them break through to the next level. Answers should be written on paper as well as shared aloud.

5. Discovering the Word: Jabez Protection

Turn to page 37 in your Prayer of Jabez Workbook.

- **1 Corinthians 10:12 – 13.** Read this passage together and refer to the workbook's summary. During this study we want to review the dangers of temptation and the methods of escape. The first question emphasizes that service doesn't exempt us from temptation, but actually attracts it. The devil focuses his attention on those who are making a difference for God.

- **Question 2.** Struggling with temptation makes us feel all alone. Yet we're fighting battles that many others are facing. This should give us encouragement and motivation to persevere.

- **Questions 3.** This question appears obvious, but the point is that strong faith in God's character gives us the strength to pass any test. We know He won't let us fail.

- **Questions 4.** First, we can ask God to show us the escape. We can ask Him to give us strength. We can use common sense, and consider the price of giving in. We can trust other believers to hold us accountable.

- **Questions 5.** Some will be uncomfortable here. Don't force anyone to share embarrassing personal information and respect their levels of comfort in being open. Your people can certainly pray for each other and encourage each other to win out over evil using biblical principles.

6. Praying Together

As this is your final formal Jabez meeting, your prayer should offer closure of the learning experience and ook forward to the excitement ahead in the Jabez life.

Homework Use the prayer of Jabez every day—for the rest of your life! Trust God to bless you, enlarge your territory, keep His hand upon you, and keep you from temptation. This is an assignment for all of us from now until eternity.